KidLit-O Presents

Career As A Police Officer

What They Do, How to Become One, and

What the Future Holds!

Brian Rogers

KidLit-O Books

www.kidlito.com

© 2013. All Rights Reserved.

Cover Iamge © Kakigori Studio - Fotolia.com

Table of Contents

About KidCaps

KidLit-O is an imprint of BookCaps™ that is just for kids! Each month BookCaps will be releasing several books in this exciting imprint. Visit are website or like us on Facebook to see more!

A police officer dressed in his uniform with all of his equipment[1]

---

[1] Image source: http://www.wonderful-words-for-a-weary-world.org/TEENS-file/images/policeman.jpg

Introduction

On March 5, 2001, the small town of Santee, near San Diego, California, suffered a terrible shock: a student at the local Santana High School brought a gun to class and began to shoot at his fellow students. Two police officers who were visiting the school that day were able to radio in for help, but there was little else that they could do by themselves. The young man was firing his gun wildly at anything that moved. How could just the two of them possibly stop the shooter and protect the innocent students and school staff that were panicked and running all around the school? The officers would have to be brave and wait for help to arrive.

Emergency response teams from the surrounding area (including paramedics, firefighters, and Sherriff's deputies) quickly arrived on the scene and blocked off the streets so that no one could get into the school or leave it without their permission. Then, a second group of officers rushed into the school and started evacuating some of the students. They had already discovered that the shooter was acting alone and was hiding inside a bathroom, so they were able to sneak out some of the students and teachers through an exit far on the other side of the building and take them to a nearby restaurant where they could meet up with their families.

In the meantime, a third team of officers stormed the bathroom where the shooter, 15 year old Charles Andrew Williams, was hiding. He tried to kill himself as the police entered but wasn't successful. After Williams was taken away to be questioned (and to make sure that he was, in fact, the guilty person), the police officers who stayed at the school knew that they still had a lot of work to do. The students who had been in the classrooms near the bathroom where the shooter had been hiding had stayed inside the whole time, too afraid to go out into the hallway. Now it was time for them to go home. The officers also had to search the area and make sure that there were no other dangers at the school- like traps or hidden bombs. Using specially trained dogs, the officers searched the shooter's locker, back pack, and other pertinent areas. Then after releasing everybody, the San Diego SWAT (Special Weapons and Tactics) team was called in to officially clear and assess the area.

Since the shootings had happened in more than one area of the school, the whole school was turned into a big crime scene. Officers were brought in to examine almost every square inch of the place looking for clues and evidence. In the end, it was discovered that the shooter had sent fifteen people to the hospital and killed two more, both students. But were it not for the quick action of the police officers and their bravery, the numbers could have been a lot worse. In other words, even more people could have been hurt and died.

Can you imagine how you would have felt if you had been asked to stop Charles Andrew Williams? Would you have been too afraid to rush into that school or would you have focused on the innocent people trapped inside and the best way to help them? Well, the police officers who were called to help that day didn't think twice: they had sworn to dedicate their lives to protecting the innocent and that's what they were going to do. And we all can be thankful that they did. Today, the shooter is behind bars, and he can't hurt anyone else.

In this handbook, we will be looking closer at the extraordinary type of person who has what it takes to become a police officer. Not everyone has the courage and quick thinking ability to stop the bad guys and to help the good guys. However, thousands of men and women across the country have decided that they are the exception and that they are willing to do the job. What do you know about being a police officer? Have you ever seen a police officer hard at work? Do you know any police officers personally?

We will look at the career of a police officer from seven different angles so that you can learn as much as possible about this important job. It will also give you a chance to see if you have what it takes to put on the uniform yourself and to get out there and help the community in this special way.

In the first section, we will talk about what the job of being a police officer involves. Along with protecting people from bad guys, police officers also work with lawyers to bring the criminals to justice. They investigate crimes and even try to stop crimes before they happen. But did you know when the first official police officers started serving, and how much money they make per year? You'll find out in the first section.

Then, in the second section, we will talk about the training process to become a police officer. Most people know that police officers must attend a special academy, but not everyone knows what new recruits learn while there. But did you know that recruits are also encouraged to go to college before attending the academy? And do you know anything about the long process between graduating from the academy and starting work as an officer? We will see in the second section.

The third section will answer the question "Is being a police officer an easy job?" As you can imagine, the answer is no. Being a police officer is extremely challenging. From the moment they put on their uniform in the morning until they go to bed at night, police officers must deal with some seriously tough things, including bad people and violent crimes. Even the training is hard. Can you guess what percentage of people start training to be a police officer but never finish it? We will find out.

Then the fourth section will show us what an average day is like for a police officer. What kinds of problems do they assist with, how long are their shifts, and how do they feel at the end of each day? You will get to spend an average day with a police officer and see what it's like first hand.

Then the fifth section will take an honest look at why not everyone is cut out to be a police officer. There are some majorly difficult things that police officers have to see and do as part of their job. They must use weapons to stop criminals, and they have to be ready to shoot their gun at the bad guy to protect innocent bystanders. But with all that power comes a lot of responsibility; officers must be careful not to abuse their power and must be willing to deal with the worst kind of people in the community, day in and day out.

The sixth section will be hugely exciting and will talk about what the future holds for police officers. Will we still need police officers in ten years or so? What will their jobs be like? Will there be any new technologies to help them be more effective at protecting the communities that they serve in?

Finally, the last section will talk about the things that you can do right now to get ready for a career as a police officer. After you have looked at this exciting career and all that challenges that come with it, if you think that you are still up to the task then this section will give you a practical list of five things that you can do in the meantime to get ready. Even though you are still a kid, there is a lot you can do to educate yourself and to prepare your mind and body for a career of being a police officer.

Police officers are an vital part of any community. After reading this handbook, you will surely appreciate them and the job that they do more than ever and maybe you might even want to become one yourself. Let's start our consideration by learning more about what police officers do for us every day.

Chapter 1: What is a Police Officer?

A police officer uses their training and tools to protect people and property[2]

---

[2] Image source: http://blogs.lawyers.com/wp-content/uploads/2012/10/Police-officer-aiming-gun-v2-300.jpg

Most likely, you have seen police officers as they go speeding down the road in their cars, with their lights flashing and siren blaring. Officers use these lights and sirens whenever they must get to an emergency in a hurry. Have you ever wondered why police officers have to drive so fast sometimes or where they are going to? Let's learn a little more about this exciting job.

Although most governments throughout the years have always had some form of law and order in their communities, most of the time there were no full-time security officers. Most often, people in the past would simply use soldiers to help maintain the peace and older judges or politicians to investigate and crimes or complaints. But as cities grew larger and the weapons carried by criminals got more dangerous, it was clear that most cities would need some sort of permanent group of people to protect them. The first official organized group of peace officers working for the government was

in London, England in 1749 and was called the
Bow Street Runners.

The Bow Street Runners[3]

While they did not patrol the streets like modern
police officers, the Bow Street Runners did work
directly for the courts of London and worked
hard to track down and arrest those who were
wanted for crimes. As you can see in the picture

---

[3] Image source:
http://georgianagarden.blogspot.com/2009/10/bow-street-runners.html

above, the Bow Street Runners carried particular sticks that to help them to defend themselves and to subdue (to bring under control) anybody who gave them problems.

It wasn't long before other cities got the same idea, and soon local, state, and national governments were all forming special police organizations to protect their citizens and to find and arrest criminals. Today, police officers have a massive responsibility on their shoulders each and every day that they go to work. Their first priority is always to protect the innocent, and their second is always to stop and arrest the bad guys. But that's not all that police officers do.

After a crime happens, specially trained police officers look for clues that will help lawyers prove to a jury or a judge that the suspected person is guilty. They may search for something as small as a hair or a fingerprint or for something as large as a murder weapon. Then, after speaking to everyone who saw the crime (witnesses) or knows something about it, the police will look at phone records, emails, pictures, security camera footage…whatever it takes to try and find out who was with the victim or who was near the scene of the crime when it happened.

Modern police officers also spend lots of time out on the streets patrolling, trying to stop crime before it even happens. Whether they are walking or using a special vehicle, they try to always let the world know that they are nearby and ready to help at a moment's notice. Police officers work closely with different agencies of the government to keep their citizens safe from terrorists. They might search suspicious people to make sure that they don't have any weapons, use dogs to try to find bombs, and spend long hours watching suspects to make sure that they don't do anything bad. When police have to watch a suspect (whether from a car, an apartment, or from far away using secret microphones), they call it "surveillance". Sometimes, a surveillance assignment (or "stakeout") can be pretty boring and the police officers working must spend many hours just waiting for something to happen. Do you think that you would get bored on a stakeout?

Police officers don't make a whole lot of money, at least nothing like doctors and professional athletes, but they do make enough to support themselves and maybe a family. The average new police officer can expect to make around $50,000 per year. However, if they study hard at college they go to the police academy, then they will have a good chance of getting promoted later on, which will, of course, mean more money in their pocket.

Overall, police officers spend most of their time protecting others. Whether they are at their desks filing reports, patrolling the streets of our neighborhoods, or bringing a criminal to justice by testifying in court, we could never imagine life without these brave men and women.

Chapter 2: What Is the Training Like to Become a Police Officer?

Recruits training to be police officers[4]

In the picture above, new recruits who hope to become police officers are taught how to subdue a suspect. It is part of their training at their local police academy. While the course only lasts about four months in most areas, the training at a police academy is intense and includes both time in the classroom and time in the gym with

---

[4] Image source: http://tinyurl.com/pk5lm6d

hands-on practice. Along with learning the basics about the rights of citizens (called "civil rights"), the recruits must learn the specific laws that apply in their jurisdiction, or the area where they will be assigned to work.

The classroom education makes it clear that, as representatives of the government, police officers must be sure that they never use their authority to break the law. Even though they may not always agree with everything that their fellow citizens say and do, they must try their best to remain neutral (not taking sides) and only worry about upholding (supporting) the law.

The hands-on portion of the training teaches the police officers how to deal with subjects who want to run away, how to help injured citizens and fellow officers, how to perform first aid, and how to handle the different types of weapons that an officer must use each day. Not only do most officers still carry night sticks (like the Bow

Street Runners used to) but they also use one or more firearms, Tasers, pepper spray, and non-lethal bullets (which means they only stop suspects and don't kill them). Recruits also learn the basics of traffic control, self-defense, and tactics for effectively patrolling the streets.

After recruits have finished their time in the academy, one of two things happens next: either they are offered a job from a police department who liked their performance during the academy or they will go around and start getting themselves interviews for jobs in one or more local departments. For most new recruits looking for a job, the first step is usually a written test. Each police station uses their own specific test, but most base theirs off of something called a Civil Service Exam. The test is multiple-choice and asks questions about the law and about what the recruit would do in certain situations.

If the recruit does well on the written test, then the next stage of the hiring process will need to be passed- a physical test designed to make sure that the future police officer can run fast enough and far enough to catch the bad guys, even if they have to wrestle with them a bit first. Called the POPAT (Police Officer Physical Abilities Test), the officers must prove that they have the strength needed to get the job done. What kinds of exercises are included on the test? While each police department has slightly different tests, the Springfield, IL Police Department POPAT gives us a good idea of what each recruit across the country will be required to do.

In less than six minutes, the recruit must run ¼ mile over a course that includes stairs, turns, hurdles, and other obstacles. Then they must use equipment to prove that they can pull and push certain amounts of weight, do some difficult jumping exercises, and then drag a human-sized dummy 50 feet. Only if they complete all of the exercises within the allotted time will they be able to move on to the next phase of the hiring process, the oral examination.

After passing the oral examination, the recruit must pass a lie detector test to verify basic facts about themselves (like who they are, what their personal history is, etc.) before going to see two doctors for a physical exam and a psychiatric evaluation. Then a full background check will be performed, which makes sure that the recruit doesn't have any serious money problems, arrest records, or problems on their driving record. Finally, the recruit will have one more interview, usually with the local chief of police or a high-ranking officer.

Why do you think that so much training and testing is required for each new police officer? Well, think for a moment about the awesome responsibility that each officer carries on their shoulders. They are expected to save the lives of others. Even when a person is suspected of doing something horrible, police officers must treat each person with respect as if they were innocent. The police officers are not judges; they are simply one part of the legal system. The last thing that they want to do is make a mistake that could end up setting a guilty person free.

We call the police in the darkest moments of our lives, like when we have a robber inside our house or when there has been a terrible accident. We want to know that the people who respond to our phone call have received the best training and are equipped with the best tools to help us in our time of need. Really, would you want police officers to be any different?

Chapter 3: Is Being a Police Officer An Easy Job?

Do you imagine that police officers just sit around and eat donuts all day?[5]

---

[5] Image source: http://thepolicedaily.com/images/donut.jpg

Sometimes, movies and TV shows make local law enforcement officers look like they spend a lot of time just standing around talking, relaxing at their police stations, and eating donuts in the local diner. In real life, however, nothing could be further from the truth. Police officers work extremely hard to protect the people and property in their communities.

The reality of being a police officer hits many recruits once they start the training. As we saw in the previous section, training to be a police officer starts with three or four months spent at the local police academy, after which the recruit must pass a series of tests. How many people successfully finish the whole process from start to finish? Less than 2% of all recruits (about 1 out of every 75) will complete the difficult training process to become a police officer.

Those who have finished the training show that they understand how serious it is to be a police officer. Almost right away, most new police officers will be assigned to work patrolling a certain area of their community. Sometimes they are assigned to work alone and sometimes they are assigned to work with a partner. Either way, they are expected to work different shifts around the clock. Because police officers are part of a workers' union, they are protected from working too many hours without extra pay. Even so, the hours they are assigned sometimes fall in the middle of the night. After all, police officers need to be ready at any time for an emergency, even if it is at two o'clock in the morning.

Another challenge that comes with being a police officer has to do with the two extremes of the job. In one day, things can be terribly scary and dangerous one moment and then boring the next. For example, police officers might have to burst into a bank to stop a gunman from shooting innocent customers in the morning, and then in the evening they might have to sit on a stakeout for hours on end waiting for something to happen. But even if they are on a stakeout, they can never really relax because the action might start at any time.

Along with the moments of action and stakeouts, police officers must learn how to deal with stressful situations. Often, they are the first on the scene of an accident or a fight, and they must help to calm everyone down and to break up the fighting. They must learn to ask the types of specific questions that get them the information they need to find and arrest the bad guys. Sometimes, they must make terribly sad visits, like when informing someone that a member of that family whom they know and love has died in an accident.

Police officers also have to be exceptionally good at expressing themselves when writing reports and filling out forms. After each call that they answer and each arrest that they make, a complete report has to be filled out and sent to the proper people. Officers often spend long hours writing each and every detail that they can remember and writing it down as part of a report. Later on, these reports will be used by lawyers and judges to decide what should happen to the guilty person.

As they work each shift, police officers have a lot of happy times, but they also see some very sad things. They see people die after car accidents and crimes, they talk to victims of robbery, and they try to comfort families who are looking for missing relatives. Throughout the years, some of the stress from the job kind of builds up inside some officers, the same way that it does for some soldiers who are fighting in a war. Each year, many police officers are diagnosed with Posttraumatic Stress Disorder (PTSD), which is a condition that makes them flash back in their minds and relive some of their worst experiences. In the most extreme cases, a few police officers have ended up hurting themselves or people that they love in moments of panic and confusion.

As you can see, being a police officer has some very real challenges to it and is by no means an easy job. Police officers must stand up to very scary people sometimes, even when everyone else is running away. Instead of spending their days eating donuts and relaxing, like the movies would have us believe, police officers are extremely competent professionals who spend their days being brave and protecting their communities so that the rest of us can live our lives in peace.

Chapter 4: What Is An Average Day Like for a Police Officer?

Some police officers ride horses during their shifts[6]

Police officers fill lots of different roles in their departments across the country. There are commissioners, chiefs, and lieutenants who work in offices and direct the activities of the officers who work out in the streets. There are detectives

---

[6] Image source: http://images.publicradio.org/content/2008/09/01/, 20080901_horses_33.jpg

who work hard to track down murderers, kidnappers, and drug dealers. There are even officers who go undercover and take on secret identities to try and catch criminals in the act of doing something bad! But the most common type of police officer (and the one that you have probably seen the most) is called a patrol officer. Let's see what an average day is like for a patrol officer.

Police officers usually work rotating shifts, which means that one day they will work while the sun is out and that the next shift won't start until nighttime, and the shifts usually last for eight or so hours. In big cities, it is not uncommon to see some patrol officers walking while others ride around on horses, which help them to keep control of large crowds control and to have a good viewpoint of what is going on around them. Near some beaches, police officers often ride bicycles; while, in smaller towns, many officers work without a partner and have their own car (which they usually take home at night).

But no matter what vehicle they use or the size of the city they work in, how do police officers spend their time during their shifts?

The first priority for a patrol officer is to answer all the emergency calls that come over their radio. Each call may be something as serious as a shooting or as simple as one neighbor complaining about another's loud music. In every case, the dispatcher will ask an officer (usually the one who is nearest to the area) to respond and to take care of the problem. The officer will go, speak with the people involved, interview witnesses, write down what they say, and make sure that everything has calmed down before they leave. Then, they must fill out the paperwork on that specific incident before heading back out on patrol.

During some shifts, the police officer spends most of their time answering one call after another. Or if one of the calls is decidedly complicated (like a murder or a terrible car accident) then the officer might end up spending a long time just taking care of that one situation. But during other shifts things may be much quieter and there may be very few (or even no) calls to go on. So how will the officer spend their time if there isn't anyone calling with an emergency?

During a quiet shift, the officer can often choose to patrol the streets of the community, looking for traffic violations or for anyone that might need their help, like when a car has broken down on the side of the road, and the driver needs help. But that's not the only way that police officers spend their time.

Do you remember all of the training that a recruit has to go through before he or she can become a police officer? They must spend weeks and months learning about the law and about practical abilities-like using weapons and arresting suspects. Well, once they have become official police officers, these men and women must continue training themselves from time to time, to make sure that they don't lose any of their valuable skills. For example, police officers must take courses about different important procedures, about how to use certain types of weapons, and about how to drive certain types of emergency vehicles.

During other shifts, officers also visit local schools from time to time to educate the students their about different subjects. Sometimes they talk to the students about how to fight against the pressure to use drugs. One such program is called D.A.R.E. (Drug Abuse Resistance Education) and it helps to prepare kids for the times when others might try to get them to smoke cigarettes or marijuana. Have you participated in the D.A.R.E. program?

Or officers may talk to students about the dangers of joining a gang. One such program, which is popular in big cities, is called G.R.E.A.T. (Gang Resistance Education and Training). The police officers who participate in G.R.E.A.T. want the best for the kids whom they talk to and don't want any of them to get into trouble at a young age or to ruin their futures.

At the end of their shift, whether it was spent answering calls, filing paperwork, visiting schools, or receiving extra training, police officers are usually pretty tired. After checking in one last time with headquarters and helping the next shift of officers to get ready for the day, they go home and rest, satisfied that they were able to help out so many people in just one day.

Chapter 5: What Is the Hardest Part of Being a Police Officer?

When you think of a police officer in your mind, what kind of a person do you think of? Do you imagine someone who is a big goofball and who doesn't take anything seriously? Of course not. Most police officers are truly serious individuals. Of course, they must be serious to deal with a lot of the bad people that they come across in the line of duty. But many police officers are serious for another reason- because of stress.

As you know, communities are made up of all kinds of people, and most of them are people who try to obey the law. There are doctors, lawyers, teachers, construction workers, students, and politicians. Most people in your community probably work hard to provide for their families and to help the whole town grow and to be a safe place. However, in every town and city, there are also a few bad guys who don't want to obey the laws and do what's right. They want to sell drugs, steal things, and hurt people. While you get to meet all kinds of people every day, police officers don't always have that choice; often they spend most of their time dealing with bad people. What effect does spending so much time with bad people have on some police officers?

While each person is different, some police officers have said that they start to look at the people around them differently. After seeing how some people that seemed to be "good" did some downright awful things in secret, some police officers start to look at everybody around them as if they were criminals. Some of them have even had trouble trusting members of their own family and think that their husband or wife is keeping secrets from them.

Another difficult part of being a police officer has to do with using the weapons that they carry. Police officers are often called into the tensest situations, where the decisions that they make can literally be the difference between life and death. Sometimes, there are terribly bad people in the neighborhood, and they only way to stop them from hurting others is if the officer uses lethal force- in other words, by shooting that person with a gun. Do you think that you have what it takes to be able to shoot another human being? Most people could never imagine doing something like that, but police officers must be ready to make that extreme decision each and every day of their lives. And even if they shoot someone in self-defense or to save the life of an innocent person, some police officers keep thinking about what they did for years, thinking about the person that they killed, their family, and how things may have been different. It is as if some officers were carrying around a heavy suitcase with them wherever they go.

Police officers have one final challenge, although most officers handle it really well. They have to fight hard not to abuse the authority that they have been given. People look up to police officers and expect them to set a high standard and to always obey the laws that everyone else must obey. But sometimes, when a person is given authority, they let it kind of go to their head and make them act a little crazy. Some police officers have gone too far when arresting a suspect.

For example, on March 3, 1991, a Los Angeles resident named Rodney King was arrested after running away from some LAPD officers in his car. When the officers finally got him to stop, four of them roughly threw Mr. King to the ground and began to hit him very hard with their nightsticks while other officers stood nearby and did not try to interfere. A nearby citizen happened to videotape the arrest and footage of the beating was shown around the country on the news programs. When the four officers weren't punished for what they had done, the African American community in Los Angeles began to riot and over 50 people died in the violence.

Police officers across the country learned a valuable lesson: being too harsh with suspects- even if they are behaving badly like Mr. King was- is never an option. Police should always act like professionals even when they are being provoked and the other person is trying to make them angry.

Each of these challenges (dealing with bad people every day, being prepared to use lethal force, and not abusing their authority) is a terribly real condition that each police officer must learn how to deal with if they are to be successful.

Chapter 6: What Does the Future Hold for the Career of a Police Officer?

In ten years or so, maybe around the time that you might think about starting of the path to be a police officer, what will the job be like? Well one thing is for sure: the world will still need police officers to keep law and order and to help protect us. While a lot of things will have gotten better by then, it is not likely that crime will suddenly disappear. But what kinds of new technologies will police officers be using? Let's look at a few.

This small device will help police during high-speed car chases[7]

One of the new devices that will probably be used more in the future is a small GPS dart (as seen above) that can be shot from a police car during a high speed car chase. Instead of risking the lives of innocent drivers on the road, the police officer can simply shoot the tracking dart onto the suspect's car and then the dispatcher can use it to follow the suspect wherever they run away to. That way, no innocent people get stuck in the middle of a dangerous chase.

---

[7] Image source: https://www.starchase.com/products.html

A special camera can protect police officers from suspects who tell lies [8]

As we saw earlier, police officers must deal with some pretty bad people sometimes. When they stop a driver for being behind the wheel while drunk or for breaking a traffic law, sometimes the

[8] Image source: http://www.taser.com/products/on-officer-video/axon-flex-on-officer-video

suspect makes up stories to try and get the police officer in trouble. However, new technology will soon make something like that a thing of the past. As you can see in the picture above, police officers will soon be given the option to record their daily activities with a special camera that they wear on their head. The bad people who might otherwise make up lies to hurt police officers or get them in trouble will soon find out that the video camera will have recorded everything and that the truth will be known. The maker of the camera says that 93% of complaints are usually dismissed when there is video, so that should help police officers to focus on doing their jobs and not on worrying so much about what lies bad people might make up about them.

Other new technologies being planned include computer programs to carefully study crimes in a certain area, like a specific neighborhood, for example. A computer can often look at and analyze much more information than a person can, which means that they can often see patterns that most people miss. It is hoped that a specially-designed computer program could analyze a certain part of town and find patterns. For example, a program might help police to learn that more crimes tend to happen at a certain time of month and during a specific time of day. Once they have that information, police officers can make sure that they will be in that area to possibly even prevent a crime before it even happens!

Other new technologies of the future will help police to control crime. Some of them will try to use a little bit of psychology to make the bad guys less likely to do bad things. For example, do you think that the color of street lights can make a difference in the amount of crime in a city? Well, in Tokyo, Japan, and Glasgow, Scotland, authorities installed blue street lights and noticed that there was an immediate drop in crime. It seems that the calming color of blue made people less likely to do something violent. This idea lets police focus on patrolling more and makes the city safer.

Another interesting method that might be used to reduce crime in the future is the use of talking surveillance cameras. Instead of a security camera that only records what's going on, cities like London, England, and Detroit, Michigan, have begun to install cameras that will allow an operator looking through the camera to speak directly to the people they sees. For example, if a crime is happening (or about to happen) the operator can speak to the people on the street and tell them to stop what they are doing or that police are already on the way. This invention can help to protect people on the streets of big cities. While some folks feel that they are losing their privacy, others feel that it is worth it to feel safe.

Other future inventions include new scanners to find footprints, tire tracks, and freshly-dug graves that can't be seen with the naked eye. Other inventors are working on cameras and radios for police dogs that will allow them to get into areas where officers can't go and still carry out their missions. But perhaps one of the most exciting new inventions is a completely new type of police car.

This is a car designed exclusively for police officers[9]

[9] Image source: http://www.autoblog.com/photos/carbon-motors-e7/#photo-1338864/

One of the difficulties that many police departments have is making sure that their officers have the right type of vehicle for the job. In many cases, this involves purchasing an ordinary car and attaching all sorts of peculiar equipment to it, because unlike firefighters, garbage collectors, and construction workers, police officers don't have cars made especially for them and their needs. That may change in the near future. The picture above shows one company's idea of how unique cars could be made just for police officers. The idea is to give them all of the tools and equipment that they need from the very moment that the car is made instead of trying to squish it all in later.

Along with all of the other exciting technologies planned for the future, which include special sensors to find traces of bombs and other dangerous items, these tools will make sure that police officers are able to handle any threat that comes their way. While their job will continue to be difficult, and there will still be plenty of bad guys out there, the new technology will make sure that police officers can do an even better job keeping us safe.

Chapter 7: How Can You Get Ready Now to Become a Police Officer?

Kids graduating from a youth police academy in their area?[10]

In most areas, new recruits must be at least 21 years old before they can apply to attend a police academy and begin the training to become a police officer. But in the meantime, that is, during the years until you turn 21, is there anything that you can do to get yourself ready for

---

[10] Image source: http://www.cranford.com/police/display.asp?choice=10

this exciting and important career? Absolutely. Let's look at five things that you can do right now to get ready.

1) Prepare your mind. Most police stations require that new officers take at least a few years of college before they can get a job. While most new recruits might choose to study a subject like Criminal Justice, any amount of time invested in educating yourself will show a police department that you are a serious person who knows how to set a goal and fulfill it. College education is also important if you want to be promoted as a supervisor later on.

Being a police officer also means knowing how to communicate well, whether when reading, writing, or conversing. So learn now how to express yourself clearly. When your teacher gives you writing assignments, try to do a really good job on them. When you have to read a long book for English class, learn to enjoy the act of reading and focus on how much you learn. And when you have to resolve problems with your friends or family members learn to how to keep control of your temper, even when things are tense. These qualities are essential for any good police officer.

2) Get involved in the community. Police officers spend their days helping their communities. So why not start doing the same thing now. Although you shouldn't try to patrol any neighborhoods on your own or anything dangerous like that, why not try to be a positive influence in your neighborhood? Volunteer at a community center, maybe as a lifeguard, organize a youth sports program, or tutor kids after school.

Another great way to help your community is to stay out of trouble. By not doing drugs or breaking the law, you make your community a safer place, let the police focus on stopping the bad guys, and give younger kids a good role model to follow. Plus, when you apply for a job as a police officer later on, you won't have a bad reputation or any problems in your file.

3) Get in good physical shape. Do you remember the impressive physical test that all recruits must pass before they can get hired as police officers? As you can imagine, all of the running, jumping, and climbing is devilishly difficult for some people. So why not start training now? Try to remember that you are training, not just to pass the test, but to be able to do the job day in and day out. Sometimes, police officers have to chase suspects, break through doors, and wrestle with criminals in the line of duty. Having a strong body helps them to be successful, and sometimes just seeing a police officer in good shape is enough to make some criminals think twice before starting any trouble.

4) Learn how to use new technology. As we saw in the previous section, police officers can expect to use lots of new technologies in the near future. Along with basic computer skills (like typing and using the internet) they will be expected to use new gadgets and tools to track down bad guys and their weapons. So, start learning now about the basics of computer use. Learn to navigate the internet and to find information quickly. Pay attention when others want to teach you something new, as you never know when you might use that information.

5) Spend time with real police officers. There is no substitute for the real thing, so why not try to talk to some police officers in your area about what it takes to do their job? Ask them why they became police officers, how the reality matches up with their expectations, and what advice they can give you. If possible, try to schedule something called a "ride-along", where you can actually spend time with a police officer during their shift and get a front row seat for life as a peace officer.

Did you see the kids in the picture at the beginning of this section? They all graduated from something called a youth police academy. They were able to spend several sessions with real police officers, getting a bit of advanced training that would help them reach their goals later on. Why not ask your parents or a trusted adult to take you to the local police station to see if they have a similar program? You may be surprised to find out that there are other kids just like you who want to become police officers. You can help each other to stay focused along the way!

Even though you may still have quite a few years until you turn 21, there is a lot that you can do in the meantime. Stay focused on your goal, and soon you will be able to serve your community as a police officer.

Conclusion

Wow! We have learned a lot of fascinating things about the career of a police officer. While most people know that police officers catch the bad guys, most of them don't know all of the hard work that goes into their job! What was your favorite part of this handbook? Was it when we learned about the difficult training or was it when we saw the exciting new technologies that will be used soon by police departments everywhere? There were so many fascinating things. Let's review some of the main points that we learned so that we don't forget them.

In the first section, we talked about what the job of a police officer involves. Along with protecting people from bad guys, police officers also work with lawyers to bring the criminals to justice. They investigate crimes and even try to stop crimes before they happen. Other police officers investigate crime scenes and look for clues as to who the guilty person was. Did you see when the first official police officers started serving? They were the Bow Street Runner in 1749, in London. We also saw how today the average police officer starts out making around $50,000 per year, although they can get raises over time and as they get promotions.

Then, in the second section, we talked about the training involved to become a police officer. Many people know that police officers must attend a special academy, but not everyone knows what new recruits learn while there. Do you remember what kinds of things recruits learn at the police academy? They learn about the laws that they have to enforce, how to control suspects when arresting them, and how to handle the different weapons and tools that they will be assigned as police officers. After graduating from the academy, recruits must pass a series of tests and exams before being hired and starting work as officers.

The third section answered the question "Is being a police officer an easy job?" As you saw, the answer is most definitely "no". Being a police officer is hugely challenging. From the moment that they put on their uniform in the morning until they go to bed at night, police officers must deal with some seriously tough things, including bad people and bad things. Even the training is hard. Do you remember what percentage of people start training to be a police officer but never finish it? That's right: less than 2% of those who start the training go all the way through and finish it. We also saw some of the unique challenges that come with being a police officer, like working strange hours, spending a lot of time filling out reports and dealing with the stress of the job.

Then the fourth section showed us what an average day is like for a police officer. We saw how their shifts are spent mainly answering emergency calls as they come in and patrolling the rest of the time. We also saw how police officers visit schools and take training courses when they aren't on the street patrolling or answering emergency calls.

Then the fifth section took an honest look at why not everyone is cut out to be a police officer-there are some extremely difficult things that they have to see and do. They must use weapons to stop criminals, and sometimes they have to be ready to shoot a gun to protect innocent bystanders. They have to be careful not to abuse their power, and they have to be willing to work closely with the worst of the worst, day in and day out. While being a police officer is an extremely noble and important job, not everyone can put up with the stress that comes with the job. If you choose to be a police officer, then it is reasonable to be prepared for both the good days and the bad.

The sixth section was hugely exciting and talked about what the future holds for police officers. Will we still need police officers in ten years or so? The answer, of course, was yes. Even though technology will help us solve a lot of problems, crime will most likely still be around by the time you are old enough to become a police officer. But we saw that several new technologies (including GPS darts, special cameras, and custom-built cars) will make the job of a police officer more exciting than ever and will allow them to keep our streets safer than ever before.

Finally, the last section talked about the things that you can do right now to get ready for a career as a police officer. We saw five practical suggestions to help you get ready before you apply for the police academy. You should prepare your mind by doing well in school and trying to get some college experience under your belt. Then, spend time with real officers, train your body, stay out of trouble, and get involved in your community. All of these things will help you to get ready.

Even though it is a job with some scary and some sad moments, being a police officer is one of the best jobs that you could choose. Not only will you be satisfied each day after work, but you will know that the entire community appreciates your hard work to keep them safe.

We saw an example in the introduction of a school shooting in California. Can you imagine how much worse it would have been if the police had not shown up quickly to evacuate the students and to stop the shooter? We can be sure that our lives are safe and happy today because the police help to keep the bad guys under control. So if you think that this is the career for you, then start getting ready: we need you out there protecting us!

Can you be a police officer in the future?[11]

11 Image source: http://how2becomeanfbiagent.com/wp-content/uploads/2011/11/Police-Officer.jpg

Made in the USA
Middletown, DE
10 January 2018